Shiver Me Chicke

A Guide to Successful and Sustainable Animal Husbandry in Zone 3

By Suzanne K. Peterson

2015 Edition

Copyright © 2015 Suzanne K. Peterson
All Rights Reserved

ISBN-13 978-1505996203
ISBN-10 1505996201

All Feedback Welcomed on **suzannepeterson83@yahoo.com**

ACKNOWLEDGEMENTS

I would like to thank all of the members of my family for their help in getting this book published:

To my parents David and Betty for their time in editing and reviewing this book

To my brothers Richard and Randall for their patient review and inspiration

To my children David and Rebecca for correcting my grammar and helping me with the nuances of the information age

I would also like to thank my fellow farmers Vonda and Greg Schiebout and Laura Dykstra for sharing their experiences with me and for their insight and encouragement.

Dedication

This book is dedicated to my grandpa, Herbert Stroschein, whose gentle manner and love for his animals is an inspiration to all who knew him.

DISCLAIMER: Although this book has useful information about keeping your animals healthy and safe, it is not a substitute for veterinary attention when it is needed. Also, animals die sometimes despite your best efforts to keep them alive. The author takes no responsibility for the health and safety of your animals. This book is intended as a helpful guide, and the rest is up to you, the owner.

Preface

For many, the idea of sustainably raising livestock in the Upper Midwest, especially in Zone 3, is intimidating. Some farmers have had limited success, while others have failed miserably. It just seems that the animals don't produce or grow like one had hoped they would.

This book holds many possible solutions for the challenges of successfully and sustainably raising livestock in a Zone 3 climate. There are successful farmers in this part of the U.S., and indeed in many other parts of the world with a similar climate. Most of that is due to adequate planning and realistic expectations.

Shiver Me Chickens is a step by step guide for planning and raising animals successfully despite the variable and in some ways extreme weather conditions. It will help the novice farmer to focus on caring for animals which require less attention and that will fit into their plan for increased self-sufficiency. It will reveal how long it really takes to raise livestock in this climate, allowing for realistic expectations. It will explain simple and inexpensive means of getting the very best out of the animals. And, by following the instructions in each chapter, it offers an easy to understand planning process to help ensure a thriving and rewarding animal husbandry experience.

How to Use This Book

Each chapter of Shiver Me Chickens can be read independently and used on its own merit. Following the instructions from beginning to end will allow any farmer to develop and put together a viable animal care plan based on the animals they want to tend. Terms which might be unfamiliar are marked with an asterisk and the definitions are given in the Glossary in Appendix F.

Chapters 11 and 12 contain additional information for those who want to know more about dealing with difficult weather conditions and animal interactions. Chapter 13 is a compendium of handy tips and tricks used by successful farmers in Zone 3. Using one or two of these tips alone could save an animal's life, and make their care a pleasure rather than a nightmare.

Table of Contents

Appendices

Figure 1 Harry the Yak Bull in Winter with Beauty's Daughter in Background

Chapter 1 Background and Intended Audience

This book is intended to provide guidance for anyone interested in raising their own source of meat, milk, fiber*, or eggs in the Zone 3 climate. Whether as a hobby or in order to provide a high quality source of food, animal husbandry is an insightful and rewarding experience. Special challenges are in store for people who live in Hardiness Zone 3, however. The temperature and humidity extremes bring extra difficulties to successfully raising animals.

In my own experience, I am drawn to raising animals because of the special kinship we can share. The day to day routine of their care, their (seemingly) endless antics and facial expressions, and their gratitude at sharing being alive with you are part of the priceless benefit of raising livestock. This connection with other living things is a strong part (for me anyway) of what I find so rewarding. You can enjoy this gift of life, and I encourage you to appreciate its wonder.

Animals specifically covered in this book include: chickens, ducks, geese, rabbits, goats, pigs, sheep, and cattle. Other animals mentioned include: yak, llamas, donkeys and guardian dogs. All of them can be successfully and sustainably raised in our widely varying climate, although certain times of year require much more labor and feed costs than others for their care.

Zone Definition

The USDA (United States Department of Agriculture) has divided the various areas of the U.S. into hardiness "Zones" based on coldest temperatures experienced during the year. Most of the Upper Midwest is in Zone 3 (minimum temperature -30F to -40F) or Zone 4 (minimum temperature of -20F to -30F). See the USDA Hardiness Zone Map in Appendix A. States with significant Zone 3 or 4 regions include: Montana, Wyoming, North Dakota, South Dakota, Minnesota, and Wisconsin. Parts of upstate New York, Vermont, New Hampshire, and Maine on the eastern seaboard also are considered Zone 3. Farmers outside of the US who work in a similar climate include those living in parts of Russia, China, and Canada. A detailed worldwide hardiness zone map is available at: **http://tcpermaculture.blogspot.com**.

A Brief History of Animal Domestication

People have been raising and caring for animals in order to harvest what they supply since the beginning of civilization. In fact, domestication of animals (and plants) is one of the chief drivers for the rise of civilization since it provides a stable food supply.

Dogs were the first animals specifically raised by people. The first animals domesticated for food were sheep (in the Middle East), then goats, pigs and cattle. Domestication of draft animals, cats, silkworms, and poultry followed soon thereafter. By approximately 1000 BC, all of the major animal types currently used by people had been domesticated – initially in Europe, Africa, and Asia, and later North and South America. Many animals were subsequently transported to other places in the world as people immigrated to new and different lands.

As modern societies have developed more efficient means of raising animals, fewer people are involved in their care. In only a couple of generations farming went from being the occupation of a majority of the people to something less than 3% of the population in modern societies. This is a shame, since caring for creatures (and raising your own food or fiber*) can be an extremely rewarding experience, both emotionally and financially.

Now that you have a bit of background on animal domestication, it's time to talk about what specific plans you have for your livestock.

Chapter 2 Begin at the Beginning: Purpose and Goals for the Animals

It is extremely important to have a plan prior to obtaining any animals. The weather can be very unforgiving, and it is wrong for an animal to suffer due to poor planning. These creatures depend on you – the owner. This sacred responsibility needs to be taken seriously, as their life truly is in your hands.

The first question to ask when considering getting livestock of any kind is what goal you have in mind. Is the animal for meat, milk, fiber*, or eggs? What are your expectations for production? How many eggs? How much meat? How much fiber*? This will help determine the number as well as the type of animals to consider. The more detailed your goals, the better you can plan to achieve them.

Animal	Product	Amount/time	Number needed

The table in Appendix B gives a summary of typical production available for common types and species of animals in a Zone 3 climate. Note that production varies significantly according to time of year and how the animal is housed. This information is based on my experience as well as that of other local farmers. Your experience may be very different because animals and conditions vary considerably. This is part of the joy as well as the frustration of caring for living things.

A couple of other important considerations: do you actually like the type of animals you are planning to raise, and will you be able to have them butchered and eat them if their purpose is meat? These may sound like simple questions, but they definitely need to be considered if you want the best chance at success.

If you don't like the type of animal you are planning to raise, you will find it much more difficult to take proper care of it, and it will quickly become a chore instead of a pleasant task. Go visit a farm that has your type of animal and make sure you actually like it before bringing one home. Talk to someone who has them and get an idea of some of the unique characteristics of the particular type of animal you want. Unlike plants, animals can move and definitely have personalities. Their successful care requires a lot more preparation than caring for plants.

Some gentle souls grow so attached to their livestock that they cannot bear the thought of their demise. Please give this serious consideration if you have any doubts. It can be very expensive indeed to keep feeding a 500 lb pig simply because he is a pet!

You also need to seriously consider that if your animal is ill or injured whether you will take it to a vet. Vet bills can be expensive and if you are raising your animals for a meat supply perhaps a $150 bill for a chicken makes no sense. On the other hand, if the chicken is truly special to you then the money may be worth it for the companionship the creature brings. Deciding this in advance should make the decision easier later if it arises.

Children are amazing about their ability to care for something knowing that it will be in the freezer later. But, like adults, there is a great variation in that ability. It is crucial to speak with your own children about the raising of animals and where meat comes from. I would suggest that you be open and honest about this aspect of animal husbandry as it applies to your situation. Just as meat from the store came from an animal that was once alive, so does the meat you raise at home. In my opinion, it is unfair to your child to hide the fact of your livestock's ultimate purpose, if it is to be eaten by the family eventually. This can serve as a marvelous lesson about life and where our food originates.

My own children have been involved with caring for our livestock all along, and they have proven quite capable of handling the fate of the animal when the time comes. It gives them an even greater appreciation for life (I think) and we all share in the joy of caring for a living creature.

Chapter 3 Fences make Good Neighbors and so do Good Neighbors

It is vital to know the local ordinances regarding types and numbers of animals you are allowed to keep. Some areas even require the signatures of most of your immediate neighbors. There should be no question as far as complying with local zoning laws. You need to be in compliance! If your local zoning regulations don't allow the type of animal you want to raise, then do your civic duty and work to change the ordinance before getting one. Trying to change the rules later usually doesn't work and the associated fines can be very expensive.

Once you know the local regulations, you should check with your neighbors anyway if they are within 100' of where you intend to keep your animals. Talking to them may provide a connection and build the local community - something which is certainly lacking in many places. It can also prevent problems later, since they won't be surprised to hear a hen* cluck or a goat bleat at 2AM.

For the sake of your animal's safety as well as your neighbor's garden you need to build an adequately sturdy fence that will contain your creatures. Certain types of animals are very good at getting out of inadequate enclosures, and you are likely to find them in your neighbors' flowerbed contentedly munching your neighbor's favorite flower! Goats are notorious for this behavior, but I have known sheep, pigs, and cattle to do at least as much damage in the same amount of time. Although not as destructive, chickens can also scratch out an entire bed of freshly planted flowers in short order while looking for bugs. Ducks and geese leave large enough droppings behind that your neighbors won't appreciate their visits either. Rabbits won't leave big messy piles behind, but they will munch off the tops of their favorite garden vegetables.

Now that you know the importance of keeping your animals at home, let's talk about fences and which types will likely work best for your animals.

COMMON FENCING TYPES AVAILABLE

Chicken Wire – lightweight mesh best used for chickens or other birds once they are a couple of months old

Welded Wire – sturdy fence capable of containing any livestock - typically 2"x4" rectangles with fencing of various heights available – 48" tall fence is an absolute minimum for sheep, goats, or cattle – pigs can push up the bottom to get out of this type of fence unless an electric fence is strung in front of it

Figure 2 2x4 welded wire fence with electric wire above it

Woven Wire (Field Fence) – cheaper than welded wire with 4"x8" rectangles that can move along the wire – adequate for cattle, but young sheep and goats can get through it easily – cattle also sometimes push it down from on top (usual height is 47")

Hog Panel – heavy duty panel 16′ long with small holes at bottom and bigger holes toward the top – either three or four feet tall – pigs cannot bend it to get under it but grown pigs can climb the 3′ panel, and younger pigs can climb up and get out the holes.

Figure 3 gate with hog panel inside to contain lambs and kids

Cattle Panel – heavy duty panel 16′ long with 4″x6″ openings all the way up – typically 4′ tall – young sheep, goats, and pigs can get through the holes, but they cannot bend it to get under or over it.

Figure 4 heavy cattle steel wires with cattle panel lining it to contain older lambs

Barb /Barbless Wire – single strand of wire with the barbed version having barbs every 6″ or so to keep animals from rubbing up against it - often used with an electric fencer – three or four strands at heights from 6″ to 4′ needed for cattle, 5-7 strands needed for sheep, goats, or pigs

High Tension Wire – heavy duty wire used with an electric fencer – wires are held in place better than typical barb or barbless wire – usually used for cattle

Electric fencer – device used to send periodic (or continuous) shocks through an electric wire to deter animals from touching or crossing it

Electric netting – portable fence used with an electric fencer for goats, sheep, or birds

Bird Netting – lightweight fine mesh netting used to keep birds from flying out of the top of the fence

Many farmers use only electric fence for their animals and have been very successful at keeping them contained. They check the fence frequently (at least weekly and usually daily) and immediately repair it if a problem is found. Electric fence is definitely the cheapest option for keeping your animal home. Realistically speaking, though, expect that at some point some animal will get through it.

For my sheep, goats, and cattle I prefer to use a physical fence (4' tall 2x4 welded wire has worked the best for me) and then add a line of electric fence either above it (to keep the animals from reaching over and pushing down the fence) or about 18" off the ground and 6" in on the animal side of the fence (to keep them from pushing out the bottom of the fence).

For pigs I use only hog or cattle panel, and usually they are also inside another fence for when they do get out (and they most likely will get out at some point because pigs are constantly digging up the ground and pressing the fence). Pigs generally prefer the neighbor's yard to yours, and it is embarrassing to have to go and retrieve them. They do, however, usually come home at night so sometimes you can lure them into a barn with grain or milk. They are pigs, after all.

For older chickens and ducks, 6' high chicken wire with bird netting covering the run has been the best option to keep them contained. I use the 6' fence so I can stand up when I am in their run. The run needs to be cat (and fox and skunk and mink and weasel and raccoon) proof if you want any eggs.

Because I am not close to any of my neighbors I have the luxury of allowing my birds to be free most of the time. This allows them to find their own food and to eat up the bugs and ticks in the farmyard. This is NOT an option for people who live in town, however. I do occasionally lose a bird to a predator, but the quality of the meat and eggs is so much better that I am willing to take the loss.

Young birds need more protection from the local cat population, so raise them in a tote or water tank with a fine mesh wire (1"x1" is adequate) on top. They also require additional heat, so a light bulb or heat lamp can successfully be set on top of the wire mesh to help keep them warm. Once they are big enough (one third to half grown) they can be moved to the adult bird facilities. NOTE: Cats can reach into a wire mesh cage up to 6" and pull out young chicks for a tasty snack. The chicks don't know to stay away from the edge of the cage, either, until it is too late.

I keep my geese in a pasture with a 4' tall fence. Geese are big enough to scare (or hurt) children, so I don't want them loose in the yard like my ducks and chickens.

My rabbits are kept in hutches off the ground and completely surrounded in fine mesh wire (1/2"x1/2" on the bottom and 1"x 2" everywhere else) because of the local cat population. And I surround the cage with something solid when a doe* has young ones. Cats can reach into that mesh cage up to 6" to pull out the babies. Rabbits can be allowed to be loose inside a run similar to chickens or ducks, but the area must be cat-proof, and the fence needs to go underground at least a couple inches to keep the rabbits from digging under it.

Figure 5 commercial rabbit cage, NOT Cat proof

Regardless of what you choose for containing your animal, make sure to account for gates and any odd corner that needs to be closed off. Animals will find a way out over time, and once that starts it is challenging to convince them that they are not allowed to be so free. They will keep trying to get out until they stay in long enough to forget.

My tallest dairy cow, Goody, will sometimes push down the top of a fence (reaching over to get the nice grass) until it is low enough for her to step over it. Once she has been brought back into the pasture, she will go right back to that spot and try again. Although it makes it easy to find where she got out, it can be quite annoying. It is good that she is so tame and easy to retrieve, but the fence destruction gets expensive.

Once you have investigated the types of fencing available, you need to calculate how much fencing you need and then estimate its cost. As a rule of thumb, posts need to be placed every eight to ten feet for woven or welded wire to maintain the fence's integrity and prevent livestock escape. Even electric fence should have posts at least every 20' or so. Portable fencing has its own post spacing requirements, so check with the manufacturer to make sure you are installing it properly. Remember to include at least one gate if you want to get your animal out without lifting it over the fence!

Write your calculations and cost estimates down. You will need this information when you put your plan together in chapter 10.

Chapter 4 Sneaky Little Devils: Small Livestock Accommodations

All animals need a place which is dry and protected from the wind. (Young animals need additional protection, which I will discuss in Chapter 8, Babies!) They can handle the extreme cold as long as they have an area where they can use their body heat to keep themselves warm. They will need extra food, however. In the heat, moving air is helpful – but plentiful cool water is essential. The most difficult times from a disease perspective are when their outdoor area is wet and the weather is warm enough for germs (and parasites) to proliferate. Young animals are the most vulnerable to this kind of stress.

This chapter discusses housing for chickens, ducks, geese, and rabbits.

Housing for Chickens

Chickens prefer to roost about 1-1/2' to 2' off the ground. You can build them a place to roost in their coop, or they will try to create their own by flying up into the rafters. Most adult chickens are able to fly up to 15' in the air, which can make their chosen roosting place very inconvenient. This may be problematic if you need to catch them.

If you are planning to collect eggs, a commercially available nesting box will work well as a warm place to stay inside the coop, but it is expensive. Depending on how many chickens you have, you can build your own box. Chickens will often lay eggs in the same box, so one nesting box per chicken is not usually necessary. You should probably have one box per three hens*, though.

Additional resources for coop and nesting box designs are listed in the Resources for Animals and Supplies in Appendix D and the Bibliography in Appendix E.

Once you have decided how you will be housing your chickens, calculate the estimated cost. You will need this information when you put your plan together in chapter 10.

Housing for Ducks

Ducks need a dry draft-free place just like chickens, but because of their larger body size they are less likely to need a heat lamp for warmth in the winter. Designs for a duck palace (coop) are quite similar to a chicken coop, and ducks will roost in the rafters if there is no suitable lower location. Unlike chickens, some ducks can actually fly some distance, and they will roost in trees overnight if left outside.

Most ducks like to nest on the ground, but they will roost at night like chickens when they are not on a nest. They also do ok with a nesting box designed for chickens, although the ducks are usually larger so a larger nesting box is necessary. They also appreciate access to a pond or even a kiddie pool in the summer. They will splash and play in the pool and generally make the water dirty, so you need to empty and clean it frequently in the summer.

In the winter, you need to be careful not to give them such a large water container that they could accidentally freeze in it. Warm water once a day, especially when it is cold, is very important. They will splash about with their bills and spill some of it, so make sure you don't accidentally make them an ice rink!

Additional resources for design of a duck palace can be found in the Resources for Animals and Supplies in Appendix D and the Bibliography in Appendix E.

Once you have decided how you will be housing your ducks, calculate the estimated cost. You will need this information when you put your plan together in chapter 10.

Housing for Geese

Geese are similar in size to ducks, but unlike ducks they generally do not like to roost off the ground. They should be provided with a dry place out of the wind and weather. They are relatively hardy, and usually handle cold better than other birds. It is possible to house ducks and geese together relatively easily, but you will need to be aware of their differing characteristics. Geese need more greens in their diets and ducks need more protein, so their growth might be slowed by raising them together.

Geese also appreciate a pond in the summer, but they are less likely to swim in it than ducks. They will make the water messy, however, so you need to plan to clean their pond frequently.

Geese also like warm water in the winter. Just like ducks, it is important that you give them enough to drink but not enough to swim in. Finding a goose frozen in a pan of water you thought too small for them to enter can be a devastating experience, especially if the goose was unable to escape and died of hypothermia.

Geese are very private when it comes to nesting, so egg collecting from them is difficult at best. Most owners raise geese chiefly for meat for this reason. Information on building a nesting area for a goose to hatch her eggs can be found in Chapter 8, Babies!

Additional resources for design of a goose house can be found in the Resources for Animals and Supplies in Appendix D and the Bibliography in Appendix E.

Once you have decided how you will be housing your geese, calculate the estimated cost. You will need this information when you put your plan together in chapter 10.

Housing for Rabbits

Rabbits can be kept on pasture in the summer as long as they are in a predator-proof fenced-in location. They eat a variety of plants, but they especially like clover and dandelions. They will need protection from the wind, sun and rain and really appreciate cool water when it is hot.

In the winter they can be kept in individual cages somewhere out of the wind. Rabbits are solitary creatures and don't mind being alone. In the winter they require fresh water once a day. In the winter, I keep my rabbits in raised cages (for ease of cleaning) with mesh bottoms and an attached windproof box. The cages are kept inside another unheated building for convenient access. I know of other rabbit keepers whose cages are completely outside (along with an attached windproof box full of straw for each rabbit).

For many growers, commercially available cages are the simplest alternative, and if you only have a few rabbits, they make sense. Especially if you are planning to breed your rabbits, specially built commercial cages and nesting boxes are available to handle the tiny helpless babies which need so much protection in order to survive.

Even with something designed specifically for rabbits, you will need to consider your individual animals. Dwarf rabbits are very small and can escape more easily than you may realize, and some of the giant breeds are so large that they will bend the bottom of the cage because of their weight.

Additional resources for rabbit housing can be found in the Resources for Animals and Supplies in Appendix D and the Bibliography in Appendix E.

Once you have decided how you will be housing your rabbits, calculate the estimated cost. You will need this information when you put your plan together in chapter 10.

Chapter 5 Contain the Beasts: Large Livestock Accommodations

Large livestock require protection from the sun (in summer) wind, water, and cold. They are amazing in their ability to handle the variations in temperature in Zone 3, but all of that comes as a stress on the animal. Poor accommodations result in slower growth weights, lower birth weights in the spring, and generally weaker animals. That needs to be taken into consideration when calculating the cost of housing. Animals discussed in this chapter include: sheep, goats, pigs and cattle.

Housing for Sheep

In the heat of summer, sheep need shade and plenty of fresh water. In the winter they need protection from the wind and snow, and access to water at least once a day. They appreciate warm water in the winter, but won't drink as much as in the summer. A draft free barn is ideal, and they will stay healthier if the barn is uninsulated (it gets too humid with so many animals in an enclosed insulated space). When lambing season comes, heat lamps or mats might be needed for weak newborn lambs*. Sheep will also survive without shelter in the winter, but they will definitely not thrive. If your breed of sheep has horns, bear in mind that the rams will "ram" each other and everything else in sight during breeding season, including you. Be sure your accommodations are sturdy and you remain vigilant!

Additional information on sheep shelter design can be found in the Resources for Animals and Supplies in Appendix D and the Bibliography in Appendix E.

Once you have decided how you will be housing your sheep, calculate the estimated cost. You will need this information when you put your plan together in chapter 10.

Figure 6 Homemade Shelter for goat and sheep summer use

Housing for Goats

Goats also require shade and fresh water in the summer. They are more sensitive to cold than sheep, and require some kind of protection from the wind and the snow in the winter as well as daily access to water. They don't like being out in any kind of inclement weather and will inform you of their displeasure by a marked unwillingness to be outside. If your goats have horns, you need to take into consideration their destructive capability and also the fact that they can get their heads stuck. This can be a fatal occurrence, so please take it seriously.

Additional information for housing your goats can be found in the Resources for Animals and Supplies in Appendix D and the Bibliography in Appendix E.

Once you have decided how you will be housing your goats, calculate the estimated cost. You will need this information when you put your plan together in chapter 10.

Housing for Pigs

Pigs require shade and plenty of water in the heat of the summer. A mud bath filled daily with cold water is really beneficial since pigs cannot sweat. They also are absolutely amazing in their ability to handle cold in the winter despite their minimal hair. Pigs will burrow into loose piles of hay and can handle even extreme cold once they are large enough (at least 100 lb if alone, 50 lb if there is more than one). They also really appreciate warm water daily in the winter since cold water only makes them colder. A draft and snow free pile of hay is usually all the pigs need. They will grow more quickly, however, in a warmer location. They also need each other for better insulation so a single small pig will need extra protection from the elements in the winter.

Additional information on how to build a shelter for your pigs is available in the Resources for Animals and Supplies in Appendix D and the Bibliography in Appendix E.

Once you have decided how you will be housing your pigs, calculate the estimated cost. You will need this information when you put your plan together in chapter 10.

Housing for Cattle

Cattle raised completely outside require the least housing of any of the large livestock. This does not mean, however, that every cow does well outside. Many of the dairy breeds and any individual cows not raised outside may not be able to take the temperature extremes. You need to take this important factor into account in your planning, so you do not end up with a weak or (worse yet) dead animal. In the summer, all cattle require shade and plenty of water. In the winter, the hardier breeds of cattle can be left completely outside (with fresh water access once a day). They will do better, though with a windproof and snow free barn. And, if your goal is for a calf* to gain weight over the winter, it will pretty much need to have access to a wind and snow-proof barn at night.

Additional information on housing for cattle can be found in the Resources for Animals and Supplies in Appendix D and the Bibliography in Appendix E.

Once you have decided how you will be housing your cattle, calculate the estimated cost. You will need this information when you put your plan together in chapter 10.

Figure 7 Agapia and Eros in April

Chapter 6 Feeding and Care of Your Animals

Unlike plants, animals need daily access to salt, food, and water. Adequate planning is necessary to ensure you don't run out of feed for them. Needing to buy hay or grain in March or April can be a very expensive proposition. You may also be forced to feed them something of lesser quality which will adversely impact their health.

In preparation for winter, you should plan to buy or raise enough feed to feed all of your animals for at least seven months (28 weeks). Winter does not always last that long, but a late or wet spring will prevent you from being able to put the animals on pasture without doing significant damage to the land. And, as an additional consideration, females close to giving birth will be eating for two (or three or four) and will have healthier babies if given the highest quality feed available.

Chickens

Young chicks need more protein than older birds and should be fed a premixed chick starter (available at the local feed store and some hardware stores). They also need clean water every day, and you should clean and sanitize their waterers every few days to prevent disease. They tend to fall into their waterers, so using a pan or pail for their water may result in drowned birds. They will also need an additional source of heat because their bodies are too small to do it on their own. (More detailed information about the tender care of baby chicks is in Chapter 8, Babies.)

Once they are 4-5 weeks old, you can feed them a chick grower ration. It has slightly less protein than chick starter and more carbohydrates for energy and faster growth. About the time they are switching over to the grower, they should be allowed outside in a protected area if at all possible. They continue to need clean fresh water daily. All birds need access to grit – small stones that the birds keep in their crop* to grind up their feed. Birds allowed outside are likely to find their own stones, but it makes sense to keep some before them anyway to make sure they have plenty of access. (Imagine if you were expected to eat food without teeth, how difficult that would be.)

One important part of getting the best taste from the meat of the birds is for them to forage for bugs in the summer. If you give them all the food they want, they will sit next to the feeder and the meat will likely have inferior flavor and texture. One way to get them moving is to feed them all they want in the coop when you lock them in at night. Take away their food (but not their water) during the day when you let them out in their run. Then give them their feed in the evening again. This only works well when they can find enough to forage during the day. Regardless, they will gain weight more slowly because they are moving around more.

Full grown chickens will do best on a premixed feed meant for grown birds (sometimes called layer ration), although chick grower is an acceptable, if more expensive, choice as well. If you are keeping the birds to lay eggs, some crushed oyster shells need to be available at all times to replenish the calcium lost in egg production. They also need clean fresh water every day and access to grit.

As the weather turns colder, the birds will need additional feed just to maintain their body temperature. Eventually a heat lamp may even be needed, especially if you want them to lay eggs. They also really appreciate any kitchen vegetable scraps (peels, wilted greens, carrot ends, and so on) as well as any spoiled milk.

As the days get shorter the birds will slow down or completely stop in their egg production. You can get them to keep laying by providing them with 16 hr/day of light. They will also stop producing eggs before and during the time they molt. Molting is when the birds shed their feathers and grow new ones. They do this about twice per year.

Chickens start laying eggs at 4-10 months of age (egg laying breeds start laying much earlier than heritage or multipurpose breeds) and will give their best egg production during the first year after they begin laying. They generally prefer to lay eggs during the day, so if you let them out you may be forced to hunt for eggs. Egg production gradually tapers off in subsequent years, and most birds lay so few egg by the time they are 4 years old that they are no longer worth their keep. Of course, by then they may be dear pets. Every bird has its own personality, and you may be surprised how much you come to appreciate their individual characteristics. More information on common chicken breeds and laying characteristics is available in Appendix C.

It is important to estimate feed costs. More data on how much it costs to raise a chicken is in Appendix B. Bear in mind, however, that this number could vary significantly based on weather or individual animal characteristics. This information as well as the cost of purchasing the birds will be needed when you put your plan together in Chapter 10.

Figure 8 Duck Duck the Gray Muscovy Duck in Winter

Ducks

Young ducks needs to be protected and given additional heat just like baby chicks, although they are bigger and grow much faster. They also need a fresh source of clean water daily, and really like a small pond for swimming. The best ration for them is Game Bird Starter if a ration specific to ducks is not available. (More information is available in Chapter 8, Babies, and Chapter 11, Animal Interactions.)

Ducks can start being given Game Bird Grower when they get their first feathers, about 4-5 weeks of age. You will be surprised how quickly they grow, and how much they eat! They are amazing bug eaters. They also would benefit from grit, and do better if they can be outside. In the winter they appreciate vegetable scraps as well.

Ducks start laying eggs at 6-10 months of age, and the meat breeds of ducks tend to lay eggs seasonally. They lay at night, generally, so it is usually easier to find their eggs if you collect eggs and the birds are allowed outside during the day. Their best year for production is generally their first, much like chickens. Making oyster shells available as an additional calcium source is important for egg shell thickness. Egg production gradually decreases over time, and most ducks can be kept for 4 years successfully. The egg production slows down or stops during molting, just like chickens. Ducks are generally more mild mannered than chickens, and their calm and delightful demeanor is very endearing. More information on common duck breeds and laying characteristics is available in Appendix C.

It is important to estimate feed costs. More data on how much it costs to raise a duck is in Appendix B. Bear in mind, however, that this number could vary significantly based on weather or individual animal characteristics. This information as well as the cost of purchasing the birds will be needed when you put your plan together in Chapter 10.

Geese

Geese are the easiest keepers of all of the commonly kept birds. They grow quickly on a diet similar to ducks (but with more greens) and need less protection than either ducks or chickens. Goslings do need a place that is warm and dry, however, and usually a heat lamp is helpful for their first few weeks of life. They need fresh clean water daily as well as access to grit, and a small pond is greatly appreciated by them. It is really fun to watch them enjoying themselves in it. They should be fed game bird starter and additional greens if a starter specifically for geese is unavailable.

Once they have grown their first feathers, they should be allowed outside and given access to a pasture in addition to game bird grower and fresh water. They are naturally grazers, so fresh grass is vital to their health and growth.

Most people raise geese for meat, so the common breeds are seasonal layers. Goslings hatched in the spring are usually large enough to butcher in the fall given adequate feed. Geese can handle the cold better then ducks, but additional feed for energy is important for them to thrive. More information on common goose breeds is available in Appendix C.

It is important to estimate feed costs. More data on how much it costs to raise a goose is in Appendix B. Bear in mind, however, that this number could vary significantly based on weather or individual animal characteristics. This information as well as the cost of purchasing the birds will be needed when you put your plan together in Chapter 10.

Rabbits

In the summer rabbits can be kept outside on pasture (protected from predators) with only shade, a fresh water supply and a mineral block. Access to rabbit (food) pellets, especially for pregnant does*, ensures optimal health. In the winter they should be kept somewhere out of the wind and weather with a snug box to nestle in at night which contains hay or straw for insulation. They don't mind being alone, so individual cages help prevent disease problems. They need thawed clean water every day, pellets, and access to grassy hay. The hay is for edible fiber, so it is actually better if it is of lower quality, not purely alfalfa or clover. They also appreciate small amounts of carrots or other fresh vegetables or greens.

If rabbits are kept in cages in the summer, cool fresh water is vital in the heat. They will thrive on pellets with some hay for fiber. If they are fed pellets they do not need a mineral block since the pellets already contain adequate mineral content.

Fiber* rabbits will need regular grooming to keep their fur from getting matted. Once matted, the fur continues to grow but the matting gets ever closer to the skin and takes away its insulating value (as well as making the rabbit look and feel miserable). Additional information on common rabbit breeds is found in Appendix C.

It is important to estimate feed costs. More data on how much it costs to raise a rabbit is in Appendix B. Bear in mind, however, that this number could vary significantly based on weather or individual animal characteristics. This information as well as the cost of purchasing the rabbits will be needed when you put your plan together in Chapter 10.

Figure 9 Grunwald the Icelandic Ram

Sheep

Depending on the breed, some sheep require only shade, grass or hay, a mineral block, and access to fresh clean water. Other breeds will require a grain supplement to remain healthy. It is important to recognize that the nutritional needs can vary widely based on the breed and age of the animal in order to accurately predict how much it will cost to care for the creature. Sheep are used for either meat, milk, or fiber* (or all three). Dairy animals have the highest nutritional needs in general, followed by the meat and then the fiber* breeds.

Sheep are prone to problems with parasites because they graze closely to the ground, so frequent pasture changes are vital to keeping a flock healthy. My sheep are only on a pasture for six weeks (at most) before moving to another location. I also don't allow them back on the same pasture in the same summer if at all possible. Herbal and conventional parasite treatments are available as well. Consult your veterinarian for advice on successful treatment plans if parasites become a problem. If your sheep seems "off" be sure to pay close attention. He cannot tell you what is wrong, so it is up to you to be attentive.

In the winter, sheep need access to fresh water daily, and greatly appreciate warm water if it is very cold outside. They should be sheared in the spring prior to the advent of hot weather. Some producers shear their sheep in the dead of winter to make lambing easier. As long as the sheep have a draft and snow free location, this works well.

Milking a sheep is relatively straightforward as long as the sheep is cooperative. They have only two teats and are milked in a way similar to goats. I generally milk my sheep by hand as they give only a limited quantity of milk (usually less than a quart).

It is important to remember that a sheep must lamb* (have a baby) before she can be milked. Most sheep are milked for only four or five months after they lamb*, unlike goats or cows.

More information about using the fiber* or milk from sheep and how to milk them can be found in the resources listed in the Bibliography in Appendix E. Common sheep breeds are listed in Appendix C.

It is important to estimate feed costs. More data on how much it costs to raise a sheep is in Appendix B. Bear in mind, however, that this number could vary significantly based on weather or individual animal characteristics. This information as well as the cost of purchasing the sheep will be needed when you put your plan together in Chapter 10. Don't forget to include milking equipment costs!

Figure 10 Felicity the Alpine Goat Doe

Goats

Goats have the shortest digestive tract of any of the ruminants*, so they are the most sensitive to a poor diet. Most breeds require high quality pasture/hay, a mineral block, and some additional grain or pelleted feed in order to remain healthy and grow well.
Dairy goats have the highest nutritional needs, followed by fiber* goats and then meat goats.

All goats need clean fresh water and a mineral block, regardless of breed. They also require more protection from the elements than sheep because their hair is not as protective as sheep's wool. They can be raised outside in the winter, but their growth rate will be slower. They also appreciate warm water to drink when it is cold outside.

They are naturally browsers and will gladly eat small trees or bushes or any other number of items to get what they need nutritionally. They also prefer to stick their heads through fences to get at whatever is on the other side. This gives them the reputation that they will eat anything, but it is only because of their short digestive tract.

Like sheep, goats are prone to problems with parasites because they graze so closely to the ground. Frequent pasture changes are vital to keeping a herd healthy. My goats are only on a pasture for six weeks (at most) before moving to another location. I also don't allow them back on the same pasture in the same summer if at all possible. Herbal and conventional parasite treatments are available as well. Consult your veterinarian for advice on successful treatment plans if parasites become a problem. It is important to pay close attention if your goat seems "off" as they cannot tell you what is wrong.

Goats are probably the easiest of the livestock to become pets, once you become accustomed to their needy nature. They are smart and curious and sometimes so very aggravating, especially when they climb over a fence just to be close to you. The pastoral nature of daily milking a goat is very gratifying, and the bond developed between a goat and her caretaker is one of the reasons people can tolerate goats' more difficult characteristics. They are agile and can get out over many fences that keep in cattle. I have watched one of my goats climb over a 4' tall cattle panel to be closer to me!

Milking a goat can be done by hand or by machine. I milk my goats by hand because they have only two teats and milking by hand doesn't take all that long with the limited amount of milk. Typically goats give 1-2 quarts of milk per milking, although some dairy breeds give over a gallon.

It is important to realize that a goat must kid* before she can be milked. Most goats are milked from the time the kids* are born until two to three months before they are due again.

Information on common breeds of goats is found in Appendix C. Resources for what to do with goat fiber* and goat milk and how to milk a goat can be found in the Bibliography in Appendix E.

It is important to estimate feed costs. More data on how much it costs to raise a goat is in Appendix B. Bear in mind, however, that this number could vary significantly based on weather or individual animal characteristics. This information as well as the cost of purchasing the animals will be needed when you put your plan together in Chapter 10. Don't forget to include the milking equipment costs.

Pigs

Unlike goats and sheep, pigs are not ruminants*. They have only one stomach and their diet is closest to ours. They are omnivores* and do best with an animal source of protein. They will also devour anything in their pen which moves too slowly, so don't be surprised when their behavior seems aggressive as they try to catch an errant cat or chicken. Pigs happily devour almost anything (weeds, kitchen scraps, spoiled milk, etc.) but will grow best on a ration specifically designed for them. They also require some of the minerals in the dirt, so if a pig is on concrete be sure to give him a scoop of dirt from time to time.

In the summer, pigs can be let out on pasture, but you should expect that they will root up the ground in at least part of their paddock. I have even seen pigs with rings in their noses try to root the ground, although they won't do it nearly as much. This characteristic can be used to prepare a weed free garden bed, so give it consideration. When I put my pigs in my garden space they ate all of the quackgrass roots!

Pigs are primarily raised for meat, and a pig born in January or February will be ready to butcher prior to the onset of winter that same year. Pigs can safely be wintered in some kind of wind and snow proof shelter with a large amount of hay so they can burrow in to stay warm. They need time to acclimate, though, and will grow a thick layer of hair to stay warm if raised outside. A single pig will have difficulty surviving the cold alone unless it is almost grown. They really appreciate warm water when it is cold outside.

Pigs are the clean up crew on the farm, and they make good use of those pesky garden weeds. They are generally healthy animals, but if you notice that your pig is "off" you need to watch him closely. He cannot tell you if he is ill, so you need to pay attention to discern what is wrong.

Additional information about pigs can be found in the Bibliography in Appendix E, and common pig breeds are listed in Appendix C.

It is important to estimate feed costs. More data on how much it costs to raise a pig is in Appendix B. Bear in mind, however, that this number could vary significantly based on weather or individual animal characteristics. This information as well as the cost of purchasing the animals will be needed when you put your plan together in Chapter 10.

Cattle

Of all the livestock commonly raised, cattle are the largest but can also be the simplest to raise. Many of the beef breeds require little more than shade, water, pasture, and a mineral block – even in the winter. Dairy cattle have been bred to need a higher level of nutrition, and you should expect to feed them grain or another supplement in order for them to stay healthy and productive. Regardless, the cattle will do better if they have somewhere out of the snow and wind in the winter.

Young stock (calves less than a year old) appreciate warm water in the winter, and they should definitely have a place free of snow and wind. Very young calves may even need additional heat and/or a blanket (calf blankets are available at many feed stores). They will thrive if given a supplement specifically designed for calves.

Cows are generally healthy and most likely you will not need to call a vet for illness. You may wish to verify your cow is pregnant or when she is due, which is a good reason to have the vet check on your animal. Because your cow cannot tell you she is feeling ill, It is very important to pay close attention if you notice she is behaving strangely.

Milking a cow is a bit more complicated than milking a goat because a cow has four teats (rather than the goat's two) and she will give a lot more milk. I milk my cow by machine because of the amount of milk given (at least a gallon per milking).

It is important to realize that a cow must have a calf* (baby) before she can be milked. Most cows are milked from the time the calf* is born until two months before she is due to have a calf* again.

In addition to dairy and beef cattle, I raise yak, which are cows from Tibet. They are extremely calm, intelligent, and efficient eaters. They are the most efficient ruminants* on the farm by far, but it also takes a lot longer for them to get to butchering size. They are the only cow which also offers the owner fiber* for use in spinning* or felting*!

Additional information about common breeds of cattle is available in Appendix C. Information about uses of cow's milk and how to milk a cow can be found in the Bibliography in Appendix E.

It is important to estimate feed costs. More data on how much it costs to raise a cow is in Appendix B. Bear in mind, however, that this number could vary significantly based on weather or individual animal characteristics. This information as well as the cost of purchasing the animals will be needed when you put your plan together in Chapter 10. Don't forget to include the milking equipment costs if you are planning to milk your cow!

Chapter 7 A Big Load of Crap – What to do with your Green Gold

One of the biggest advantages to raising your own animals is the supply of natural fertilizer available to you. It is important to allow the manure to age appropriately so it does not injure the plants you are trying to feed. In particular, chicken and pig manure are very strong and need to be aged at least six months prior to application. The amount of nitrogen in their new manure is enough to burn any plants unfortunate enough to be too close.

One exception to the rule of aging your manure is to dig a trench and use it to heat a garden bed in the winter. My great grandparents used horse manure to extend their growing season. (I give more information about this technique in my first book in the series <u>Shiver Me Parsnips</u>.)

The simplest method of aging your mixture of manure and bedding from your animal's pen is to let it sit outside over the course of a season or two. This may be problematic if your neighbor's house is next to your pile. It is also important that it be downhill from your vegetable garden. Until it has aged properly runoff from your pile could contaminate your vegetables. These are important considerations for your pile's placement.

Most manure and bedding piles only have a strong smell for a week or so, unless someone digs in to them. Your pile may heat and steam (even in the winter) which means the bacteria are breaking everything down into humus* (compost). You may speed decomposition by turning the pile. This also aids in killing any weed seeds which may be in the pile from the animal's manure or the bedding.

Some things in the pile may not rot (twine and plastic are two common items found in a manure pile) so it is important to keep them out of your pile in order to make it easier to use once it is done decomposing. You also need to make sure your animal's bedding material will decompose if you want to use the manure as compost in your garden.

The pile is ready to use once it looks like crumbly black or brown dirt. The process takes 6-9 months. Decomposition does occur in the winter, but at a much slower rate than when the weather is warmer. (Note: grubs found in a decaying manure pile make great sunfish bait. If left to mature they become June bugs.)

Figure 11 Steaming Compost Heap

Chapter 8 Babies!

Chickens

Sometimes in the spring you will notice one of your laying hens* becoming very protective of her eggs. She is being broody*, and if you put the eggs from your other hens* under her she will set* them and, after 21 days or so, you may hear peeping coming out from under her wings. (This only works if you have a rooster with your hens*, however.)

The new life under the mother hen* is precious indeed, and being involved with these tiny creatures is an experience fraught with joy and sometimes sorrow. It is important to let the new chicks stay with their mother until they are completely dry and fluffy. If you have your chickens in a predator-proof location, you can even allow the hen* to raise her chicks. She will naturally do a better job of keeping them warm than you could ever hope to do. The hen* will also teach the chicks what to eat, but you may need a special small/lower waterer for the chicks so they don't accidentally drown in the hen*'s water. They will grow on what you feed the hen*s, but perhaps a bit more slowly than if they got chick starter.   If you want to ensure that your babies don't get out, you will need to baby proof your coop. This means closing any opening that chicks could possibly find to get out (less than 1/2"x1/2").

If, however, you do not have a predator-proof location, it is important to put the chicks in a predator proof location with a heat lamp. The lamp needs to be adjustable and hanging above the chicks as you will gradually be lifting it up higher until they no longer need it. You can tell if the lamp is about the right height if the chicks wander around underneath it but don't avoid it and don't crowd each other under it. About once a week or so adjust the lamp upward. By the end of four or five weeks (if the weather is mild- spring or summer) you should be able to turn the lamp off. It is important to pay attention to the chicks and check them a couple of times a day, especially in their first week of life.

If you get newly hatched chicks from a hatchery be sure to dip their beaks first in water and then in their feed as soon as you get them ready to be settled into their new home. Otherwise they may not know what to do since they don't have a mother hen* to teach them.

It is important to clean their waterers daily for the first month to minimize disease problems. You will empty, scrub, and rinse them, but don't use any chemicals lest you poison your babies! Chick feeders and waterers are available at your local feed store, probably right next to where you get their feed.

I raise my chicks in an old cattle tank with fine mesh over the top. That works until they are about 4 weeks old, then I put them in a cat proof location to get most of the way grown (12-16 weeks).

Ducks

Most likely your duck hens* will start wanting to hide and set on their eggs in the spring. You need a drake* in order for her eggs to be fertile. The time of nesting varies based on duck breed (and the weather). Ducks prefer to nest on the ground if possible, so you should set up an area in their pen for her to make a nest. Duck eggs need 28 days to hatch (35 days for Muscovy ducks), and allowing the mother to care for them works even better than for chickens as the ducks are better mothers in general.

If you get newly hatched ducklings from a hatchery be sure to dip their beaks first in water and then in their feed as soon as you get them ready to be settled into their new home. Otherwise they may not know what to do since they don't have a mother to teach them.

A heat lamp is helpful for ducklings, but they grow so quickly they probably won't need it for long. Adjust the height based on their behavior, just like chicks (see above).

It is important to clean their waterers daily for the first month to minimize disease problems. You will empty, scrub, and rinse them, but don't use any chemicals lest you poison your babies! Chick feeders and waterers can be used for the ducklings, although they would also appreciate a small pond. Because ducks can swim (and chicks cannot) usually it is best to raise ducklings and chicks separately.

Geese

Most likely your geese will start wanting to hide and set on their eggs in the spring. You need a gander* in order for her eggs to be fertile. Geese like a private place to nest, so it is important to have something set up so the goose is comfortable laying and setting* her eggs. An old tractor tire with hay works well as a nest if it is in a somewhat secluded location. Goose eggs need 28 days to hatch, and allowing the mother to care for them works even better than for chickens as they are better mothers in general.

If you get newly hatched goslings from a hatchery be sure to dip their beaks first in water and then in their feed as soon as you get them ready to be settled into their new home. Otherwise they may not know what to do since they don't have a mother to teach them.

A heat lamp is helpful for goslings, but they grow so quickly they probably won't need it for long. Adjust the height based on their behavior, just like chicks (see above).

It is important to clean their waterers daily for the first month to minimize disease problems. You will empty, scrub, and rinse them, but don't use any chemicals lest you poison your babies! Chick feeders and waterers can be used and are available at your local feed store, probably right next to where you get their feed. Goslings like ponds, too, so offering them someplace to swim is very beneficial for them.

Goslings and ducklings have different nutritional requirements, so although it is possible to raise them together you may encounter slower growing animals because of their different diets.

Rabbits

Rabbits can be bred to have babies any time of year, and they are induced breeders. This means that when you put the buck* with the doe* he will breed her, and then she will ovulate and become pregnant. It is usually best to bring the doe* to the buck* because does* tend to be more aggressive than bucks* and may hurt a buck* put in her pen.

After 30 days, the doe* will kindle*. You can tell she is close when she starts pulling belly hair to build a nest. Sometimes this is a week before she has babies, sometimes it is when they are about to come out.

It is important to have a nesting area set up for your doe* at least two weeks before she is due. A solid sided nesting box designed for rabbits with hay works well. When the babies are born, they are hairless, blind, and helpless, so a safe warm place for them is vital to their survival. The bottom of the box needs to be solid because they are so small that they will fall through any openings.

A doe* will have anywhere from three to ten babies. Generally she will appear to ignore her babies once they are born, but don't be fooled. She will go into the nesting box and feed them when they need it. Otherwise she will be nearby and may be very protective of them if anyone tries to touch them.

You should check the babies daily, and make sure their bellies are full and that they are growing adequately. They will start getting hair right away, and their eyes will open at 4-5 days. Once their eyes start to open they will try to get out of the nesting box (bunny popcorn bouncing up and down). They are still tiny, so make sure they cannot get somewhere to fall through the mesh bottom. Also, make sure cats cannot get too close to the cage. They will stick a paw in and kill any baby within reach prior to pulling it out for a snack. I put a solid wall around the cage, including the top, when a does has young babies.

If you have a bunny baby which needs to be bottle fed, be prepared for a tremendous commitment. They will need a special tiny bottle (kitten bottles work well) and to be fed every hour around the clock. They will also need a heat lamp as they cannot keep themselves warm enough.

Baby rabbits grow incredibly fast and can be weaned at 4-6 weeks of age. Leaving male babies with the mother too long may get her unintentionally bred by her own son. A doe* can be bred and have healthy babies up to four times per year

Sheep

Sheep can have lambs* any time of year, but some breeds are seasonal and will only have lambs* in the spring. A ram* is needed to breed the ewes*, and his behavior may get more aggressive during breeding season. Rams* not with the ewes* at this time will also get more aggressive and will "ram" anything – each other, the gate, you - so be especially vigilant when you are around them at this time.

A lamb* is in its mother's womb for approximately five months. When the ewe* is close to lambing she will wander around looking for and calling for her baby. When labor is intense she will lay down and push. It is best to generally leave her in peace until you see the water bag (amniotic* sac) appear. At that point, keep track of the time. The baby needs to be born within an hour of the appearance of the sack or the overly long birth process may kill it. The profit or loss for many shepherds is based on how many live lambs* they have, so they literally live with their sheep during lambing season. (Having slept in the barn across the fence from my ewes* I can assure you it is a one of a kind experience!)

For the sake of your animals, you need to educate yourself on what you should or should not do prior to the labor hour! That is beyond the scope of this introductory book, so please consult the resources listed in the Bibliography located in Appendix E.

Usually, though, the birth process is beautiful and amazing to witness. First two tiny hooves appear, followed by the nose, and then after a few pushes the head comes out and the rest of the body right behind it. If the sack is unbroken, break it open and clear the lamb's* nostrils so it can breathe. Usually the mother will turn around and start licking it off, calling to it in the special mama call you will get to recognize after hearing it a few times.

If the ewe* has twins (or triplets) the next lamb* will usually not come until 15-20 minutes later. It is important to pay attention as the second delivery will go a lot faster and often the amniotic* sac doesn't even break. Then, tragically, the second baby suffocates if mama is still busy with the first baby.

You will know the ewe* is done when you see the placenta*, which often comes out an hour or so after the last baby. She will want to eat it, which is an excellent protein source for her so let her do it. Usually you can tell if the placenta* is not out yet if there is still something hanging out the back end of the ewe*.

It is a good idea to put the ewe* and her newborns in a separate pen so they can bond. This lessens the number of rejected lambs* and allows you to verify that the lambs* nurse within the first hour or so after birth. Unfortunately, rejection is not particularly unusual among sheep, so educate yourself ahead of time on how to handle the situation.

Bottle baby lambs* should be fed at least three or four times daily for the first week, and then twice daily until they are weaned at three months. This is a significant commitment, so make sure you are prepared for the disruption to your schedule. If the lamb* did not nurse from her mother, make sure she gets colostrum* in the first 24 hours. Otherwise she will have a compromised immune system for the rest of her life.

It is important to castrate* the ram lambs* before they get too big because the bigger they are the harder it is on them. Castration* (they are then called wethers*) is important because it affects the quality of the meat at butchering time for many breeds of sheep. Some farmers also dock tails. Information about castration and tail docking techniques can be found in the resources in the Bibliography in Appendix E.

Goats

Goats can have babies any time of year, but spring is the most common time. A buck* is necessary to breed the does* and he will get even stronger smelling when breeding time comes. He can also get more aggressive, so be prepared when you go in his pen. When the doe* is in estrus*, she will allow him to ride her. He will do so many times that day, so you are likely to see it. Put the date on your calendar because she is likely to have babies five months later.

When the doe* is close to kidding* she will wander around looking for and calling for her baby. When labor is intense she will lay down and push. It is best to generally leave her in peace until you see the water bag (amniotic* sac) appear. At that point, keep track of the time. The baby needs to be born within an hour of the appearance of the sack or the overly long birth process may kill it. Goat keepers have also been known to spend a lot of time in the barn during kidding* season.

For the sake of your animals, you need to educate yourself on what you should or should not do prior to the labor hour! That is beyond the scope of this introductory book, so please consult the resources listed in the Bibliography in Appendix E.

Usually, though, the birth process is beautiful and amazing to witness. First two tiny hooves appear, followed by the nose, and then after a few pushes the head comes out and the rest of the body right behind it. If the sack is unbroken, break it open and clear the kid*'s nostrils so it can breathe. Usually the mother will turn around and start licking it off, calling to it in the special mama call you will get to recognize after hearing it a few times.

If the doe* has twins (or triplets) the next kid* will usually not come until 15-20 minutes later. It is important to pay attention as the second delivery will go a lot faster and often the amniotic* sac doesn't even break. Then, tragically, the second baby suffocates if mama is still busy with the first.

You will know the doe* is done when you see the placenta*, which often comes out an hour or so after the last baby. She will want to eat it, which is an excellent protein source for her so let her do it. Usually you can tell if the placenta* is not out yet if there is still something hanging out the back end of the doe*.

It is a good idea to put the doe* and her newborns in a separate pen so they can bond. This lessens the number of rejected kids* and allows you to verify that the kids* nurse within the first hour or so after birth. Although less common than with sheep, rejection happens with goats, so educate yourself ahead of time on how to handle the situation.

Bottle baby goats should be fed at least three or four times daily for the first week, and then twice daily until they are weaned at three months. This is a significant commitment, so make sure you are prepared for the disruption to your schedule. If the kid* did not nurse from his mother, make sure he gets colostrum* in the first 24 hours. Otherwise he will have a compromised immune system for the rest of his life.

It is important to castrate* the buck* kids* before they get too big because the bigger they are the harder it is on them. Bucks* need to be castrated* (they are then called wethers*) so the meat is not overcome by the heavy smell emitted by intact bucks*. It is also really beneficial to dehorn your goats as their horns cause all kinds of problems. Information about castration and dehorning techniques can be found in the resources in the Bibliography in Appendix E.

Figure 12 New born Piglet Pile

Pigs

Pigs can be bred to farrow* any time of year, but it is easiest on the piglets in the spring or early summer if they are born outside. A boar* is needed to breed the sows* and they will stand and allow him to breed them when they are in estrus*. Boars* are generally of a gentler nature than sows*, so usually they are not overly aggressive when a sow* is in estrus*. Still, it is always wise to be cautious around a 200 (or up to 600 lb) animal who has sharp teeth and could eat you!

Sows* are pregnant for 111 days, and usually have anywhere from 4-16 piglets. You can tell she is close when her udder* fills, and labor is imminent when she lays down and starts pushing. If she has trouble with the first piglet, the rest will die so it is really important to make sure once labor starts, each baby comes out. I do not recommend going in the pen unless it is absolutely necessary. Some very nice sows* get extremely protective when in labor or with their young pigs.

My sows* farrow* in a pile of hay and it can be hard to tell where the baby pigs are or even how many she has. Once all the babies are born, she will start to call them to her. Make sure that she is in a pen where the babies cannot get out. Especially initially they wander a lot looking for her. Depending on the sow*, sometimes she lays on a baby or two, and there is no hope for their survival in that case – they are crushed. This is why some farmers keep the sows* in a special farrowing crate so they cannot lay on their young. I have lost a few piglets over the years, but I prefer the sow* to have the freedom of movement. That is a decision you will need to make when setting up your animal's accommodations, so be prepared.

Sometimes a piglet is too weak and cannot compete with his siblings. You can bottle feed him, every 3-4 hours for the first week or so. After that, 3 feedings a day is sufficient. You will be amazed at how fast he grows, and by six weeks he can be weaned completely.

It is important to castrate* the male piglets before they get too big because the bigger they are the harder it is on them. They are called barrows* once castrated*. Information about castration* techniques can be found in the resources in the Bibliography in Appendix E.

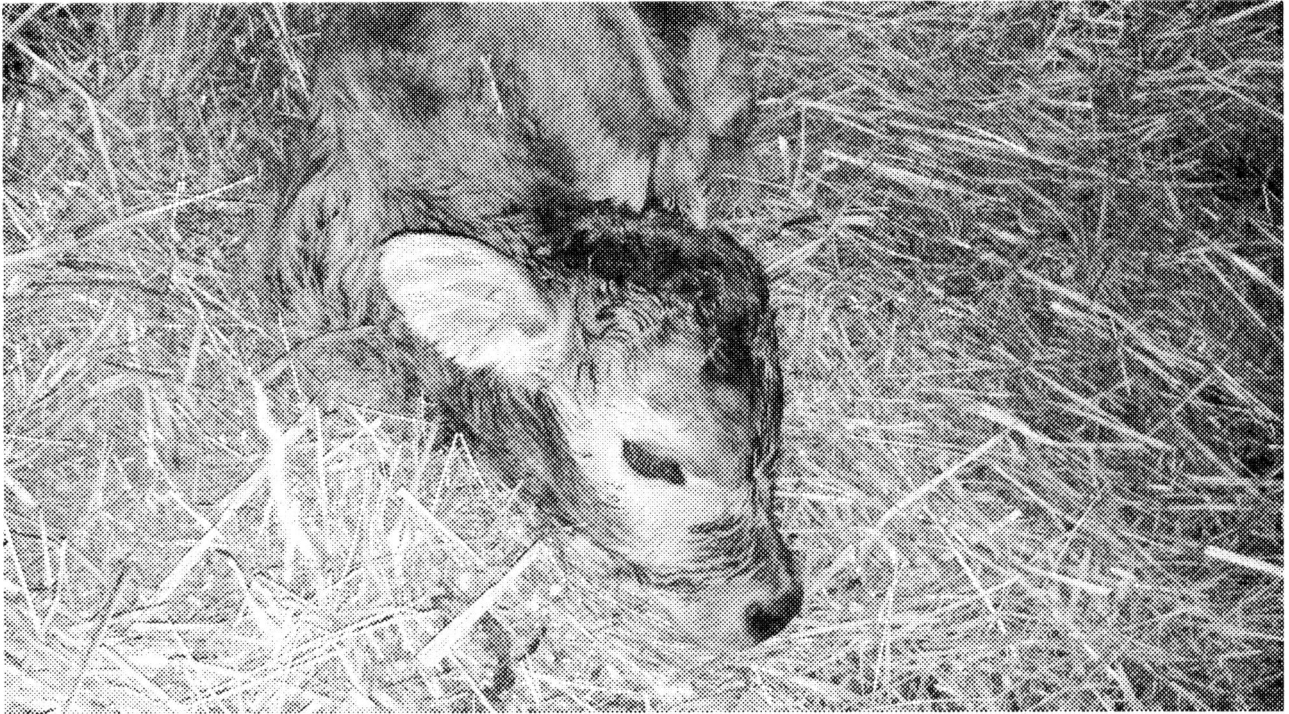

Figure 13 Newborn Faith the Dairy Calf

Cattle

Cows can be bred to have calves any time during the year. A bull is needed to breed the cows, although artificial insemination is used by many farmers because of the dangers inherent in having a bull on the farm.

The cow will stand and allow the bull to breed her when she is in estrus*. A female cow which has not had a calf* is called a heifer*. Cows cycle every 21-28 days (depending on the individual animal). If no bull is around other cows or steers* will try to breed her. This is how you know that she is not bred. Since cows have a nine month gestation, knowing when a cow has been bred is vital to accurate planning.

A cow's back end will start to loosen a month (or two for older cows) prior to calving. When she is close to having her baby she will try to find a quiet out of the way place to have it. Labor can take from 8-24 hours, so just keep checking on her. Once the amniotic* sac appears the calf* should come out in the next hour or so. If the cow appears to be having an exceptionally difficult time you may need to intervene. That is why it is important to have your cow in a place where you can observe her and help if needed.

For the sake of your animals, you need to educate yourself on what you should or should not do prior to the labor hour! That is beyond the scope of this introductory book, so please consult the resources listed in the Bibliography in Appendix E.

Usually, though, the birth process is beautiful and amazing to witness. First two tiny hooves appear, followed by the nose, and then after a few pushes the head comes out and the rest of the body right behind it. If the sack is unbroken, break it open and clear the calf's* nostrils so it can breathe. Usually the mother will turn around and start licking it off, calling to it in the special mama call you will get to recognize after hearing it a few times.

Twins are fairly rare in cattle, (and generally heifer* calves that are twins to a bull calf* are infertile) so the placenta* will likely be the next thing out. It can take up to 24 hours for the placenta* to be expelled. You can tell if it is still in your cow if she has something hanging out her back end.

The mother will usually get up and lick the calf* and nudge to get it moving within fifteen minutes after it is born. The calf* will struggle to get up (and they are so clumsy at this stage!) and eventually succeed. Mother beef cows can be extremely protective of their newborn calves, so be exceptionally cautious and gentle around them during the first week of the calf*'s life.

Rejection of the calf* by her mother is very rare, but sometimes you will need to bottle feed a calf*. Colostrum* in the first 24 hours is vital, or the calf* will be permanently weakened. Twice a day feedings are adequate for all but the smallest calves. More information about bottle feeding is available in the resources listed in the Bibliography in Appendix E.

It is important to castrate* the bull calves before they get too big because the bigger they are the harder it is on them. Dehorning is also important for both heifers* and bulls, particularly for dairy animals. Castration has some positive impact on meat quality, but it also makes the bull calf* less aggressive (once castrated they are called steers*). Information about castration and dehorning techniques can be found in the resources in the Bibliography in Appendix E.

Chapter 9 A Dose of Reality

Although caring for animals is an amazingly rewarding experience, two unpleasant truths are inescapable:

1) Animals die,
2) It will cost more to raise your animals than if you just went to the store to buy whatever you wanted to get from them.

For some people, these are strong enough negative factors that they will not even try. They truly are missing out, but I would be remiss if I did not state these facts clearly.

I think it is important to discuss both concepts. I'll start with the easier one first – cost. There is really no way to compete with the economy of scale that is offered by commercial agriculture. They have access to the least expensive feed, housing, bedding, and so on. They are designed for efficiency and to do things as inexpensively as possible. The experience of animal care and the animal interactions are not necessarily a priority. Although many animals are raised in a more limited space in many commercial scale operations, I think it improper to paint them all with the same brush and condemn them. Their purpose and your purpose are not all that different, after all. I know a number of commercial farmers who care deeply for their animals, and do everything they can to make the animals' lives as pleasant as possible. They also try to be efficient and they are very successful at balancing these seemingly contradictory goals.

For those who are not overcome by emotion at the thought of losing an animal, feel free to skip the rest of this chapter. It is meant to console, and not everyone needs consolation. (That is perfectly acceptable, by the way. My son loves and cares for animals but he needs no consolation at their demise.)

Let's talk about the other difficult topic: death. On the farm, animals die – sometimes when you plan them to (butchering), but more often at a time when you don't (lamb* born dead, chick drowned in a waterer). Regardless, death can feel devastating. To watch the life of a creature in your arms fade away is heartbreaking indeed. Many are the times I have cried at the loss of a newborn lamb* or a calf* that refuses to get up or a bird injured by a predator, especially if I had been trying to help them survive. It is important to realize that it is ok to grieve their loss. A precious and beautiful life is gone, never to return. That is true just as much for an animal sent to the butcher as it is for one that dies unexpectedly. It is part of the bittersweet joy of farming.

And, it is important to realize that you are not a failure if an animal dies unexpectedly. Especially at the beginning, there is a steep and painful learning curve. On this road, there are no shortcuts. Animals are amazing in their ability to find myriad ways to die, just as their lives are so amazing to behold. The learning never ends, and after a while you get smarter but you cannot always be successful in preserving an animal's life.

I read the following in a blog recently (**http://dykstrasfarm.blogspot.com** – used with permission and a blog I find insightful):

"And then there are days where I feel like I've failed my many farm-animal-responsibilities and there's nothing to do to reverse the situation. We discovered (too late!) that a duck was waterlogged in the small livestock trough and was probably going to die. I wrapped her up in some loose straw to pull some moisture out of her feathers and to retain any body heat. She still died. The reason? It was my fault, in a way. I moved the trough and forgot to put some rocks back in the water at one end so that a chicken or duck could get out if they fell in. Little things like that can be overlooked, and the learning is harder by trial-and-error. It really can be life-and-death on a daily basis here, and sometimes it's my fault or negligence that caused it. No-one asked what lessons I've learned along the way (all three years of it so far), but that would need to be one of them: Always think through what could harm or kill one of your animals and do what it takes to prevent that scenario. Sometimes you still can't prevent it.

What I don't understand is this: Ducks can float on ponds for hours and hours, and they have oily feathers that repel water. Why did this one get so waterlogged that she didn't survive?!!! Sigh! (For Diana and Luke: She was not one of your ducklings from last year!)

Every day it's a choice of priority, and sometimes we get it right. Other times, like moving the trough, it was the priority that day a few weeks ago, but I didn't think through the precautions that might be needed until there was a tragedy."

Here are some tips to help you deal with this aspect of livestock husbandry. Not everyone can do these things, but they do bring some degree of comfort (to me, anyway):

1) Name your animals
2) Be grateful for every opportunity for interaction including how tasty and wonderful they are on the table or in the socks you are wearing from their wool
3) Try to do as much planning as possible to avoid bad situations
4) Realize that at times ending the animal's life is the kindest thing to do
5) Learn from your mistakes and forgive yourself
6) Love them and rejoice in the privilege of your involvement in their lives and the enrichment that provides in your own life.

Chapter 10   Putting Together your Animal Husbandry Goals and Plan

Now that you have gotten a clearer picture of what it takes to raise animals, it is time to put together a plan.

Find where you will purchase your animals, whether locally or by mail for newly hatched birds. Make sure the type and number of animals you want are actually available. Some of the larger hatcheries and livestock breed websites are listed in Appendix D.

Put together a budget for any housing or fencing that needs to be done to accommodate your animal. Also plan how you will accomplish this construction. Putting up a fence in December is probably not practical, for example, although it can be done.

Gather the following information:
      Calendar that goes out at least a year (two if you are raising cattle)
      Animal Purchase Costs
      Housing and Fencing Costs
      Planned Purchase and butcher dates of animals
      Feed Costs
      Butchering Costs (if you don't do it yourself)

Enter the expected date of purchase of your animals as well as the expected butcher date, due date of any babies, and any other relevant information on the calendar.
Put the housing and fencing project completion dates on the calendar.
Any fencing and housing projects need to be completed prior to bringing your animals home, so make sure you give yourself adequate time to prepare for them.
Put the expected feed costs on the calendar about the time you plan to purchase them.

You should now be ready to go and get your livestock. Use the calendar to track your animal's progress. Then, get your animals and enjoy the opportunity to participate in caring for another living creature. It will be rewarding in many more and different ways than you can imagine!

The rest of this book has some additional information about special weather considerations and animal type interactions. There is also a chapter on interesting and useful tips, tricks, and techniques gleaned from other farmers in Zone 3.

Chapter 11   Special Weather Considerations

One of the challenges associated with the Zone 3 is the variability of the weather. Livestock are generally capable of handling the extremes, but they will do much better if you are prepared to help them handle stressful weather conditions.

Rapid Temperature Change

Especially in the late fall or early winter the temperature can drop by as much as 50F in less than 48 hours. This is especially difficult for half-grown animals, particularly birds. Usually the temperature change is also associated with strong winds, so it is important to get your animals in out of the wind. Make sure they have plenty of bedding to nestle into and be insulated from the cold. Warm water to drink is also important. Birds seem the most vulnerable to stress in these conditions because of their smaller body size.

Above/Below Freezing Temperature Swings

Cattle have a particularly hard time with this weather stressor. It is important that their hay be mold-free and any grain be very clean. Their bedding also tends to get soaked, so give them extra just to keep them as dry as possible.

Heat and Humidity

High humidity is usually associated with heat and offers an excellent breeding ground for parasites and germs. It is important that all animals' water be kept very clean and they are given plenty of fresh bedding in addition to ample water. Moving air is usually helpful for cattle, which are more affected by the heat than other livestock described in this book.

Prolonged Cold

When the temperature remains below 0F for several days in a row all livestock need extra feed just to stay alive. Give the best quality hay available to the ruminants* (cattle, sheep, and goats), and give pigs, rabbits and birds extra feed. Make sure all animals have adequate bedding and give the young cattle and other smaller animals warm water at least once a day. (This sometimes means hauling 50 gallons of warm water or more.) Put a heat lamp out for all birds and any other animal that looks stressed. Particularly animals born the previous spring will need extra help staying warm. Calf* blankets can also be used on sheep or goats that are suffering from the cold.

Heavy Rain

Heavy rain will sometimes leave major puddles in an animal's pen or even flood their shelter. It is very important to go out and check on your livestock right after a storm to make sure they have safely survived. This is particularly important when you have young birds, sheep, goats, or pigs because they are most vulnerable to drowning.

Chapter 12 Symbiotic and Antagonistic Animal Relationships

Despite what one might see on Disney movies, not all livestock should be raised in the same space. There are also some opportunities for animals to successfully share the use of a limited area.

Pigs/Birds

This is definitely an antagonistic relationship. Pigs are omnivores*, and they will try to eat anything in their pen. If the poor creature is too slow it becomes lunch. It is best for pigs to have their own space, although they can be successfully raised in a large area with cattle or sheep outside of lambing and calving time.

Sheep/Goats

This is a symbiotic relationship. They get along well in the same pasture eating different things, and at night they each go into their own groups. If the sheep go to the right the goats go to the left. It is a very interesting dynamic, and one I didn't believe until I watched it in my own animals.

Cattle/Sheep

Historically this has been an antagonistic relationship because the sheep eat everything down to the ground so that the cattle have nothing to eat. In a pasture rotation situation, however, it works well. Allowing cattle to graze first followed by bringing in sheep makes maximum use of limited pasture space.

Guardian Animals

Guardian animals such as donkeys, llamas, or dogs can be very effective at protecting livestock from predators and their company can be enjoyed as working pets. Each type of guardian has its positive and negative qualities so choosing which one is best will depend upon your needs as well as which guardian appeals to you most as an animal under your care.

Llamas and donkeys are able to graze with their herd, so no additional feeding is necessary. This makes feeding them quite straightforward. Llamas also sometimes have fine fiber* which you can spin* or felt*.

Guardian dogs, however, are often a more effective deterrent if there is a lot of pressure from wolves or coyotes. (Note: in Africa Anatolian Shepards are used to keep away cheetahs).

I have had all of these types of guardians, and I enjoyed and appreciated all of them for their protective instincts. As a general rule, guardian animals are the most vigilant and effective when they are the only one of their particular type of animal. Then the flock to be protected is considered their "herd" and they guard it accordingly. When they get another of their species, however, they now have another creature which is their "herd" and their guardianship of the flock suffers accordingly.

Figure 14 Morning's Dew the Llama guarding the sheep

Chapter 13   Tips, Tricks, and Techniques

Here is a compendium of tips, tricks, and techniques from farmers in Zone 3.

Moving animals

It is generally easier to move animals when they are calm, so try not to get overly excited when things don't go as you expect. They can read your fear or excitement clearly and will react accordingly.

Move pigs by backing them up and putting grain where you want them to go. They like to be with their "herd" so separating one pig can be challenging.

Sheep like to move as an entire herd, so bring them all in and then separate them. Otherwise, they will try to escape to be back with the one left behind.

Goats are intelligent and friendly and can be taught to come when called by name.

Dairy cows can usually be trained to come when called at milking time.

Beef cattle tend to be wild when out in the open so get them into an enclosed area prior to trying to work with them.

Twisting a cow's tail and pushing forward will often get her to move without kicking.

All animals can easily be trained to come to the rattle of a pail with feed in it if they get treats on a regular basis. This is particularly helpful when loading them into trailers.

Milking uncooperative animals

If a goat or sheep will not cooperate, tie one hind leg back or get a set of hobbles*. Hobbles* tie the legs of the goat together so she must lift both at the same time. For milking, the back legs are hobbled.

If a cow is uncooperative get her as trapped as possible so she cannot move sideways. Then use her own weight to keep her from picking up a hoof to kick by leaning into her.

A special device can be purchased that is like a giant clamp that keeps a cow from kicking. It is sometimes called a cow trainer and goes over the cow's back and clamps down right in front of the hips on top. It is very effective but promotes an antagonistic relationship with the person doing the milking.

Ways to warm animals in cold weather

If newly born or wet, rub vigorously with a towel to stimulate circulation.

Cover the whole body with straw or a blanket as much as possible to use body heat for insulation. Although covering the head is helpful, make sure the animal can still breathe.

For small animals, use your own body heat if they are chilled. Place the creature on the bare skin of your stomach or chest and hold it in your hands to cover it with warmth.

Heat lamps are also effective because of their radiant heat. It may take some time to notice, but it will definitely have a positive warming effect. Heating pads work even better for the larger animals (sheep, goats, pigs, cattle).

Use the old lining of a coat to go around your heating pad so it can be easily washed and reused, and your heating pad stays clean.

Ways to cool animals in hot weather

When it is really hot in the summer, put a bottle of frozen water in the rabbit's cage so he can nestle with something cold.

Set up a fan to blow air on any animal that seems extremely hot. This is especially important for cattle.

Create a large mud puddle for pigs to wallow in their pen. They cannot sweat, so they need to cool off by either laying in water or digging in the dirt. Moving air helps them also, but not as much as a puddle.

Ample cool water helps all animals in the heat.

In extreme heat you can spray water in front of a fan to cool the air on its way to your animals.

Bottle Feeding

Have an esophageal* tube feeder on hand to feed a very weak or sick animal. It allows you to keep the nutrients coming even when the animal refuses to drink.

Never feed an animal on its side. (Get their head up at least.) The milk is likely to go into the lungs and drown it. And once it is in there you cannot get it out and your animal dies or is severely weakened.

Never let a baby skip a feeding. If it doesn't want to drink something is wrong, so keep it at least hydrated.

Probios (probiotics) are helpful and can save costly vet bills. They resupply the bugs that may be missing in an animal's gut. They are not a cure-all, though, so consult a vet if your animal is still not behaving as you expect. It also helps to use them when getting an animal from someone else or if there is a major change to their food supply.

Cow colostrum* can be substituted for sheep or goat colostrum* if necessary. Thaw or warm colostrum* in a hot water bath, not the microwave!

Even for grassfed animals, a little bit of grain is helpful for bottle babies in getting the digestive system (rumen) established.

As far as starting a calf* on a bottle, the air hole, of course, should be up. Also, especially for calves, to open their mouths, you can go in the side behind their incisors. There is a gap in their jaw back there between the incisors and the molars. I stick my thumb in there while straddling the calf* and then stick the bottle in. I often rub the bottle back and forth on their tongue to stimulate the sucking and get them started. If they have never drunk, they can be pretty dumb.

Most animals can be trained to drink from a pail right away, rather than a bottle. The milk may not go in to the right place in the stomach, however, so although it is faster it is probably not better for the animal. This is especially true for the ruminants* (but not for pigs, who have only one stomach).

AND OF COURSE – HAVE FUN!!!!

Figure 15 Farm Sweet Farm

Appendix A USDA Hardiness Zone Map

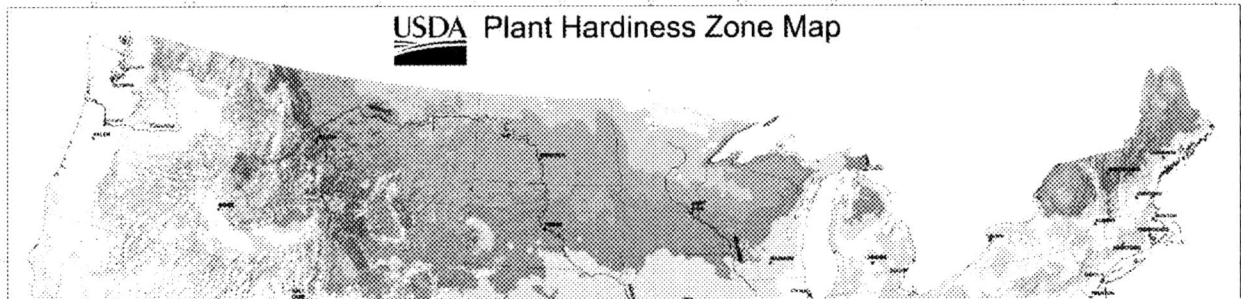

Figure 16 USDA Hardiness Zone Map 2012

Shaded areas indicate Zone 3 or 4.

WORLDWIDE HARDINESS ZONE MAP AVAILABLE AT: HTTP://TCPERMACULTURE.BLOGSPOT.COM

APPENDIX B ANIMAL PRODUCT HARVEST QUANTITY AND PRODUCTION TIME

ANIMAL	FEED/WEEK	PRODUCT	FREQUENCY	HARVEST AMOUNT	TIME TO HARVEST
COW	250 LB HAY 14 LB GRAIN	MILK*	DAILY	1 GAL	CALF BIRTH
COW	200 LB HAY	MEAT	ONCE	250 LB	78 WKS
PIG	70 LB FEED	MEAT	ONCE	150 LB	30 WKS
GOAT	50 LB HAY 3 LB GRAIN	MILK*	DAILY	2 QT	KID BIRTH
GOAT	35 LB HAY 2 LB GRAIN	MEAT	ONCE	25 LB	40 WKS
GOAT	35 LB HAY 2 LB GRAIN	FIBER	ANNUAL	8 LB	ANNUAL
SHEEP	35 LB HAY 3 LB GRAIN	MILK*	DAILY	1 QT	LAMB BIRTH
SHEEP	35 LB HAY	MEAT	ONCE	25 LB	40 WKS
SHEEP	35 LB HAY	FIBER	ANNUAL	6 LB	ANNUAL
RABBIT	5 LB PLTS 1 LB HAY	MEAT	ONCE	3 LB	26 WK
RABBIT	5 LB PLTS 1 LB HAY	FIBER	MONTHLY	3 OZ	18 WK
GOOSE	4 LB FEED	MEAT	ONCE	7 LB	30 WK
DUCK	3.5 LB FEED	MEAT	ONCE	6 LB	26 WK
DUCK	3.5 LB FEED	EGGS	WEEKLY	5	MATURITY
CHICKEN	3 LB FEED	MEAT	ONCE	5 LB	22 WK
CHICKEN	3 LB FEED	EGGS	WEEKLY	6	MATURITY

*THIS IS JUST TO MAINTAIN YOUR ANIMAL DURING THE TIME YOU ARE MILKING, THIS DOES NOT INCLUDE FEED FOR WHEN SHE IS PREGNANT.

THESE NUMBERS ARE TYPICAL FOR SUMMER CONDITIONS. IN WINTER, PLAN FOR AN INCREASE OF AT LEAST 25% IN FEED CONSUMPTION.

THE FEED NEEDED IS TYPICAL FOR MEDIUM SIZED ANIMALS, AND THE NUMBERS ARE MEANT TO BE CONSERVATIVE TO ENSURE AN ADEQUATE FOOD SUPPLY FOR PLANNING PURPOSES. YOUR FEED AND HARVEST RESULTS MAY BE VERY DIFFERENT.

EXAMPLE CALCULATIONS USING THE TABLE

1) How many chickens and how much feed does it take to get 12 eggs/week?

   According to the table, you will need two chickens to get 12 eggs per week (12/6= 2).
   In order to feed the chickens you will need 2*3lb=6 lb of feed per week

This is just to feed the chickens while laying. If you plan to start with day old chicks you need to account for the feed to get them to maturity also.

2) How many pigs and how much feed will it take to get 150 lb of pork?

   According to the table you will need one pig
   In order to feed the pig up to butcher weight you will need to feed it for 30 weeks at 70 lb feed per week 70*30=2100 lb of feed

This is just to get the pig up to butcher weight. It does not including butchering costs.

3) How much feed does it take to get 7 gallons of milk per week from a cow?

   According to the table you need one cow.
   In order to feed the cow you need 250 lb of hay and 14 lb of grain

This is just to maintain the cow while she is milking. It does not including the feed for bringing her to maturity or when she is not being milked.

4) How much feed does it take to raise 25 meat chickens to 5 lb each?

   You will probably lose some animals, so start with 30 day old chicks
   In order to feed each one up to 5 lb butcher weight you will need 3*22 lb of feed = 66 lb per bird Using 27.5 as the average you need 66*27.5 = 1815lb of feed

   This is just to get the chickens large enough to butcher. It does not including butchering costs.

APPENDIX C COMMON LIVESTOCK BREEDS AND USES

Dairy Cattle

Holstein – 1200-1500 lb cow with very high milk production- low butterfat
Jersey – 600-800 lb cow with high butterfat content milk - docile
Guernsey – 1000-1200 lb cow with medium range milk production
Brown Swiss – 1100-1400 lb cow with high milk production – very docile

Beef Cattle

Angus – medium solid black or red with tender meat and fast growth
Hereford – medium red with white face – hardy and slower growing
Longhorn – small, very hardy and tough – very low fat meat
Scottish Highlander – medium size with shaggy hair, very hardy and usually gentle

Pigs

Hampshire – black with white shoulder stripe – big hams
Duroc – red with lots of muscle
Berkshire – heritage breed with darker meat
Red Wattler – American breed with distinctive red meat - gentle
Potbelly – Asian small specialty breed usually kept as pets (but edible)

Sheep

Friesen – most common dairy sheep
Icelandic – triple purpose sheep, lots of long wool - seasonal breeder
Shetland – hardy colorful sheep with fine wool – seasonal breeder
Dorset – medium meat sheep - year round breeder
Columbia – tall meat/wool sheep with white face – year round breeder
Hampshire – meat sheep with black face and wool on head – year round breeder
Suffolk – large meat sheep with black head – year round breeder

Goats

Boer – meat goat
Angora – fiber goat
Pygmy – small breed used chiefly for pets
Saanen – white dairy goat – high producer
Alpine - multicolor dairy goat- medium to high milk production
LaMancha – dairy goat with tiny ears – low to medium milk production
Nubian - large dairy goat with floppy ears - very high milk production

Chickens

Leghorn – small flighty very high production white egg layer
Orpington – gentle large dual purpose white or brown egg layer
Rhode Island Red – high production brown egg layer
Cornish Rock Cross – fast growing meat breed
Ameracauna – medium production green or blue egg layer
Aracauna – specialty breed blue or purple egg layer

Ducks

Muscovy- dual purpose medium duck which hisses
Khaki Campbell – high production egg layer
Rouen – giant mallard looking meat bird
Pekin – white fast growing meat bird

Geese

Toulouse – large gray and white gentle bird
Pilgrim – large bird with males and females of different colors
African – medium bird with bump on top of head
Embden – large white meat goose
Chinese – medium bird with bump on top of head similar to but smaller than African

Rabbits

New Zealand- white fast growing meat breed
California – white with brown ears fast growing meat breed
Lop – medium to large floppy eared rabbit
Angora – Fiber breed
Satin – fiber breed
Rex – medium rabbit with smooth even fur – makes beautiful smooth pelt
Flemish Giant – Extra large and gentle meat breed

APPENDIX D RESOURCES FOR ANIMALS AND SUPPLIES

ONLINE

Hatcheries and Poultry Supplies

McMurray Hatchery   **www.mcmurrayhatchery.com**

Stromberg's Hatchery **www.strombergschickens.com**

Welp Hatchery **www.welphatchery.com**

American Poultry Association **www.amerpoultryassn.com**

Rabbit Supplies

Rabbitmart **www.rabbitmart.com**

Bass Equipment **www.bassequipment.com**

American Rabbit Breeders Association   **arba.net**

Sheep and Goat Supplies

Hoegger Goat Supply   **hoeggerfarmyard.com**

Hobby Farms **www.hobbyfarms.com**

American Sheep Industry Association **www.sheepusa.org**

American Dairy Goat Association **adga.org**

American Boer Goat Association   **abga.org**

Pig Supplies

Hobby Farms **www.hobbyfarms.com**

National Pork Producers Council **www.nppc.org**

Beef and Dairy Cattle

National Cattleman's Beef Association **www.beefusa.org**

National Association of Animal Breeders **www.naab-css.org**

Purebred Dairy Cattle Association **www.purebreddairycattle.com**

OTHER LOCAL RESOURCES TO INVESTIGATE

Many times, the best information on animals and supplies is found locally

    County Extension Service (in U.S.)
    Farm Service Agency
    University Agriculture Department
    Feed Supply Store
    Hardware Store
    Pet Store
    4-H Club
    Future Farmers of America Chapter
    Local Breeder's Association

Local connections with people who are doing what you want to do can be the support network you need to be more successful.

APPENDIX E BIBLIOGRAPHY AND FURTHER READING

Church and Pond, <u>Basic Animal Nutrition and Feeding</u> Wiley and Sons 1982 ISBN 0-471-87514-7
>   College animal nutrition text – useful for determining how much feed is needed

Craig, R.A., DVM <u>Lippincott's Farm Manuals Common Diseases of Farm Animals</u>, 1919
>   Classic and thorough guide to diseases – long section on parasites

De Bairacli Levy, Juliette <u>The Complete Herbal Handbook for Farm and Stable</u> faber and faber 1991 ISBN 0-57116-116-2
>   Complete reference for herbal treatments for most livestock

Diamond, Jared M. <u>Guns, Germs, and Steel: The Fates of Human Societies</u> Amazon 1999 ISBN-13: 978-0393317558
>   Tells the story of why human societies have evolved as they have -also a PBS documentary

Kains, M.G. <u>Five Acres and Independence: A Handbook for Small Farm Management</u>, Dover Publications 1973 ISBN 0-486-20974-1
>   Guidebook for finding and setting up a small farm as a business

King, F.H. <u>Farmers of Forty Centuries: Permanent Agriculture in China, Korea, and Japan</u>, St Martin's Press 1911 ISBN 0-87857-867-6
>   Thorough study of sustainable farming practices in Asia at the start of 20th century

Lee, Andy and Foreman, Patricia <u>Day Range Poultry: Every Chicken Owner's Guide to Grazing Gardens and Improving Pastures</u> Good Earth Publications, LLC 2002 ISBN 0-962468-7-2
>   Detailed guide for a small scale commercial pastured poultry operation

Logsdon, Gene <u>Small-Scale Grain Raising</u> Chelsea Green Publishing 2009 ISBN 978-1603-58077-9
>   Guide to growing grains organically for eating or feeding livestock

Logsdon, Gene <u>The Contrary Farmer</u> Chelsea Green Publishing 1995 ISBN 093003174-1
>   Hilarious, practical and uplifting book about operating a family farm from one of the masters

MacGerald, Willis, Editor <u>Making The Farm Pay: Money Saving Methods</u>, S.A. Mulliken 1911

    A classic historical guide to farming profitably including information on building the soil, plant and animal crops, and even how to cook without wasting food

Macher, Ron <u>Making Your Small Farm Profitable</u> Storey Books 1999 ISBN 1-58017-161-3

    Guide for building a profitable farm business using the principles of sustainable agriculture and agripeneurship

Macleod, George MRCVS, DVSM, Vet., FF <u>Hom   A Veterinary Materia Medica and Clinical Repertory</u> The CW Daniel Company LTD 1983 ISBN0-85207-257-0

    Reference for common natural remedies and vaccines used in veterinary practice

Madigan, Carleen <u>The Backyard Homestead: Produce all the food you need on just one quarter acre</u> Storey Publishing, LLC 2009 ISBN 978-1-60342-138-6

    Guide to Food Self Sufficiency with good information on small scale livestock raising

Morris, Edmund Miler, Ralph C., Miller, Lynn R. <u>Ten Acres Enough: The Small Farm Dream is Possible</u> Small Farmers Journal reprint of 1864 edition with new sections 2002 ISBN 1-8852-10-03-5

    Inspiring and detailed guide to establishing and profitably operating a small farm

Nelson, Melissa, DVM <u>The Complete Guide To Small-Scale Farming: Everything You Need to Know about Raising Beef and Dairy Cattle, Rabbits, Ducks, and other Small Animals</u> Atlantic Publishing Group, Inc 2010 ISBN 978-1-60138-375-4

    Detailed guide to developing the business side of small scale livestock husbandry

Simmons, Paula <u>Raising Sheep the Modern Way</u>, Storey Communicaitons 1976, 1989 ISBN0-88266-529-4

    Thorough and conventional guide to raising sheep with a long section on fences and pastures

Spaulding, C.E. DVM, and Clay, Jackie <u>Veterinary Guide for Animal Owners</u> Rodale Press 1976, 1998 ISBN 0-87596-404-4

    Clear and understandable reference for caring for livestock and pets

Appendix F Glossary

Amniotic Sac – sack inside mother's womb that carries baby

Barrow – castrated male pig

Boar – intact male pig

Broody – bird that wants to sit on her eggs and hatch them

Buck – intact male goat or rabbit

Calf- young cow

Castrate – render a male incapable of reproduction

Colostrum – special milk provided by a mother mammal for its young right after birth

Crop- organ in birds which digests food by grinding it up between small rocks

Doe – female goat or rabbit

Drake – male duck

Esophageal Tube Feeder – special feeder that goes down an animal's throat to feed directly into its stomach

Estrus – part of the cycle where a female can conceive babies

Ewe – female sheep

Farrow – to have babies (used for pigs)

Felt – process of chemically binding fibers together using agitation, soap and water

Fiber – hair, wool, or fur grown by an animal and harvested to be used by people

Gander – male goose

Gilt – female pig which has not had piglets

Heifer – female cow which has not had a calf

Hen – female chicken or duck

Hobbles – straps used to tie together an animal's legs to keep it from getting away or moving too much

Humus – finished compost

Kid – young goat

Kindle – to have babies (for rabbits)

Kit – baby rabbit

Lamb – baby sheep

Omnivore – an animal that eats both plants and animals

Placenta – afterbirth – it feeds the baby when it is in the mother's womb

Ruminant – animal which has multiple stomachs and regurgitates food to chew it again and move it further in its digestive system

Set – when a bird stays on a nest with eggs in order to hatch young

Sow – female pig

Spin – process of twisting fibers together to make yarn or thread

Steer – castrated male cow

Udder – milk producing part of a mammal

Wether –castrated male goat or sheep